THIS WORKBOOK BELONGS TO:

_____

WELCOME TO OPEN HANDS!

Talking about money is not exactly like eating cupcakes, friends. It's more like whole grain oatmeal with blueberries: it's wholesome, you know it's good for you, but it doesn't exactly spark joy.

But here's the thing. Money is part of your life. Every. Single. Day.

Money isn't good, nor is it evil. It's simply a tool. So we want to help you learn to handle that tool. Maybe flavor up that oatmeal with some peanut butter or cinnamon spice. The Bible gives us a TON of wisdom into how finances should go and not go. We took our cues from the deity upstairs.

None of the stuff in here is groundbreaking, nor new, nor novel. It's just good, practical, and we hope we're packaging this age-old wisdom in a way that you find accessible.

No matter if you're rich or poor, full of student debt or you got off scot-free, we hope you'll resonate with some of the concepts here and encourage others around you. As Christians, we're called to be wise caretakers of our resources, and wow, what a gift we're called to take care of.

Let's do our job well, and do it wisely. Let's bless and be blessed by generosity. So we begin.

-TEAM WONG

TABLE OF CONTENTS

LAY THE FOUNDATION
INTRODUCTION TO OPEN HANDS

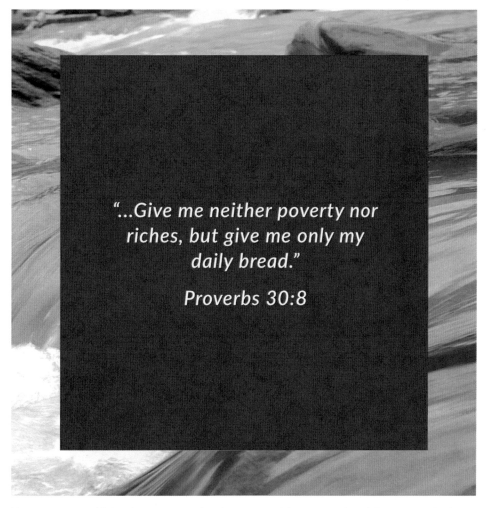

"...Give me neither poverty nor riches, but give me only my daily bread."

Proverbs 30:8

You can access additional resources and podcasts at any time at openhandsfinance.com/podcasts

10 min

INTRODUCTION

Welcome to week one. We're so excited you're joining us. Money is a big deal to talk about, learn about, deal with, and generally it requires a lot of bravery . . . so three pats on the back that you showed up.

HOW IT WORKS

To give you a quick orientation: there will be six sessions (and an optional seventh session):

- ◇ Lay the Foundation: Introduction to Open Hands
- ◇ Budgeting: Make a Money Plan
- ◇ Saving: Build a Cushion
- ◇ Debt: De-Stress your Debt
- ◇ Investing: Make Money Work for You
- ◇ Everyday Money Habits: Financial Decision-Making
- ◇ Managing Money as a Couple (Optional): Fight Less and Build your Life Together

Each session has a 10-20 minute podcast to kick off the topic; then questions, activities, and case studies in this workbook for you to dig a little deeper into the subject and figure out how it applies to you personally. By the end of the course you'll:

- ◇ Learn how to master a budget
- ◇ Be confident in your money decisions
- ◇ See money as a tool to be used wisely and generously (ok, so we can't guarantee you'll see it this way: but we hope you soak some of it in!)
- ◇ Open a Roth IRA account (if you're eligible and don't already have one). Don't be intimidated, we'll walk you through the basics!

OPENING A ROTH IRA

On that note: let's talk. You may not know what the heck we're talking about, but stay with us. A key piece of this class is for you to open up a Roth IRA. This is a type of retirement account that is particularly beneficial when you're young and at the beginning of your earning potential.

To add money to a Roth IRA, you'll need to have "earned income" the year you contribute. That could be dog walking, babysitting, pulling weeds, working a summer job—anything where you worked and got paid for it. Now, you don't have to use that money to invest, but the amount sets your cap for how much you can put into the account. Earned $350? You can contribute $350. Earned $50? You can contribute $50.

We're going to ask you to round up $100 to start one of these accounts. We'd love for you to be invested in your future (quite literally) and front your own $100, but this is a great option if you want to reach out to a family member or relative to see if they'll match $50 for your $50 if $100 is tough to swing.[1]

Alright, now let's dig in.

---

1 Some groups have a matching option built in. Your group leader will explain the details if you fall into this category. If this isn't an option in your group but you're interested in learning more, reach out at www.openhandsfinance.com/contact

PODCAST NOTES

openhandsfinance.com/podcasts

_____
_____
_____
_____
_____
_____
_____
_____
_____
_____
_____
_____
_____
_____
_____
_____
_____
_____
_____
_____
_____
_____
_____
_____
_____
_____
_____
_____
_____

PODCAST RECAP

◇ We are stewards: we're caretakers of the resources God has given us.

◇ Hold your life plans with open hands.

◇ Be intentional with your money. As Christians, we should be making shrewd financial decisions.

◇ Where is your heart? Operate with an open hands mentality.

Set timer

7 min write

10 min talk

QUESTIONS

On a scale of 1 to 10, how confident are you in handling your day-to-day money?

◇ ◇ ◇ ◇ ◇ ◇ ◇ ◇ ◈ ◇

A LITTLE
TERRIFIED

GLOWING BALL OF
CONFIDENCE

On a scale of 1-10, how intentional was your family about money/finance?

◇ ◇ ◇ ◇ ◈ ◇ ◇ ◇ ◇ ◇

DIDN'T TALK ABOUT
MONEY AT ALL

FAMILY'S HAD ME
BUDGETING SINCE I
WAS EIGHT

On a scale of 1-10, how comfortable are you in talking about money?

◇ ◇ ◇ ◇ ◇ ◇ ◇ ◇ ◈ ◇

WOULD RATHER GO
TO THE DENTIST

AS COMFY AS SOFT
HOUSE SLIPPERS

What do you want to learn from this class?

Grant - Relearn terminology

Cleto - Budget + save LONGTERM STRUCTURE

Wilfred - LONGTERM family, investing

Lily - Budget & Investing (overwhelmed)

Mary - Investing

Matthew - Application

Josiah -

Skuler -

What makes you a little nervous about this class?

Hannah - Credit Cards / Budget expectation | Investing / Bills

Jonah - Spendy | Process slowly

Jordan - Loans / Budget

William - Loans | Loans

Eve - Card terms | Unknowns

DISCUSSION

Discuss the questions above. Share as much or as little as you're comfortable with.

QUESTIONS

There were two important parables brought up in the podcast. Let's dig into those.

THE STORY OF THE WIDOW'S MITE, LUKE 21:1-4

What does it say?

_____

_____

_____

What does it mean?

_____

_____

_____

How does it apply to your life now?

_____ Give even when you don't think you can _____
_____ cause it's God's money _____

_____

_____

THE PARABLE OF THE TALENTS, MATTHEW 25:14-30

What does it say?

_____

_____

_____

What does it mean?

_____

_____

_____

How does it apply?

_____

_____

_____

_____

CASE STUDY

We've included case studies with each session to get you thinking through these concepts with real life examples. These case studies aren't designed with one right and wrong answer, so we encourage you to discuss how you would handle the situation.

JUSTIN & MARTA

24 YEARS OLD, SCIENCE TEACHER | 24 YEARS OLD, GRAPHIC DESIGNER

LOCATION	SALARY	GIVING	RETIREMENT	TAKE-HOME	SPENDING
Cincinnati, OH	$75K Combined	$600/Month	$950/Month ($425 each)	$2,825/Month	$2,250/Month

Justin and Marta are newlyweds living in the Midwest in a modest one-bedroom apartment in downtown Cincinnati. They're saving 15% toward retirement (this is set up on autopay), they give consistently (also on autopay), they don't have any credit card debt, and they're working to pay off Justin's student loan debts. They don't really worry about money, but they don't really talk about it either, it's just kind of there. They drive dependable used cars and are decidedly frugal, saving $500-$600 per month. For what? They don't really know, but they're definitely building a nice pocket of savings.

What kind of financial shape would you say Gary and Marta are in?

_____

_____

_____

Would you say Gary and Marta are living with an "Open Hands" mentality?

_____

_____

_____

If not, what would it look like for Justin and Marta to move to an "Open Hands" mentality? Do you think any of their financial choices would change?

_____

_____

_____

_____

OUR THOUGHTS

Their situation is completely understandable and often quite commendable: but we say there's something more for them! It's kind of like C.S. Lewis's quote: "We are . . . like an ignorant child who wants to go on making mud pies in a slum because he cannot imagine what is meant by the offer of a holiday at the sea. We are far too easily pleased."

Honestly, for them to move to an Open Hands mentality, I don't think we would see too much of a shift in their actual financials. They would likely save, give, and spend a very similar amount to how they are allocating their funds now. The real shift would be internal!

WHAT HAPPENS

Justin and Marta start saving more intentionally for a down payment on a house in their favorite neighborhood that they hope to buy in a few years. They've both made a point to actually understand how their retirement accounts work, and ended up diversifying their accounts further. They still give the same amount, but their generosity comes a little easier and they started serving at their church as they felt more invested in it (quite literally). Justin and Marta became less concerned with "getting rich" and more concerned about stewarding their resources wisely, and they found their financial life was a little more joyful and their brains somehow a little more content.

PRACTICAL STEPS THIS WEEK

Make a tiny financially-related goal that can be completed before the next session. Make it measurable, attainable, and timely. Here are some examples:

- ◇ Look at your student loans (knowledge is power).
- ◇ Remember your bank account password (the struggle is real).
- ◇ Buy someone a coffee.
- ◇ Eat in instead of going out.
- ◇ Tithe on your income (no matter how small).

YOUR TINY FINANCIAL GOAL

_____

_____

_____

2 min
Answer then talk

COMPREHENSION QUESTIONS

1. In the parable of the talents, what financial principle is tied to the story?
   a. Investing
   b. Saving
   c. Debt
   d. Generosity

2. How can you tell if someone has an Open Hands mentality?
   a. They give away a lot
   b. They give away 10%
   c. It depends where they give money
   d. You can't actually tell, it depends on their heart

3. Which one of these people is not legally allowed to contribute to a Roth IRA?
   a. Olivia, who will earn no money this year, but her parents will fund her account
   b. Ethan, who spends summers cutting lawns and is 18
   c. Sawyer, who ran a lemonade stand and is 8
   d. Jade, who babysits on the weekends every so often

ROTH IRA PART ONE: OPENING AN ACCOUNT

Shifting gears just a bit. As we mentioned earlier, opening a Roth IRA is a huge benefit of this class, and we're going to take the first step today. We will dig into what a Roth is during session five and why it's so great for you, but in the meantime we are taking care of the housekeeping. In this case, it's going through the (virtual) paperwork to set up an account (don't worry, you're not funding your account yet).[2]

1. Choose an account provider (we'll use Fidelity in our examples, but the choice is up to you). Look for an option with no account minimums, commission-free options, and reputable customer service. Do your own research and pick one you like best (or if you already have an account provider, they likely have a Roth IRA option).[3] Other account provider examples include:
   a. Fidelity
   b. TD Ameritrade
   c. Vanguard
   d. E*Trade

2. Set up a Roth IRA account with the provider of your choice.

3. Review and confirm your information.

4. You've set up your account, good work!

---

2 Check out the Roth IRA Setup playlist on the Open Hands TikTok account for a step-by-step guide: @openhandsfinance
3 Open Hands Finance, LLC, Rachel Wong, or Brian Wong do not make any personal investments on behalf of our readers; neither do we provide specific investment advice.

THAT WRAPS UP WEEK ONE!

Start working through your goals this week, and thanks for joining.

BUDGETS
MAKE A MONEY PLAN

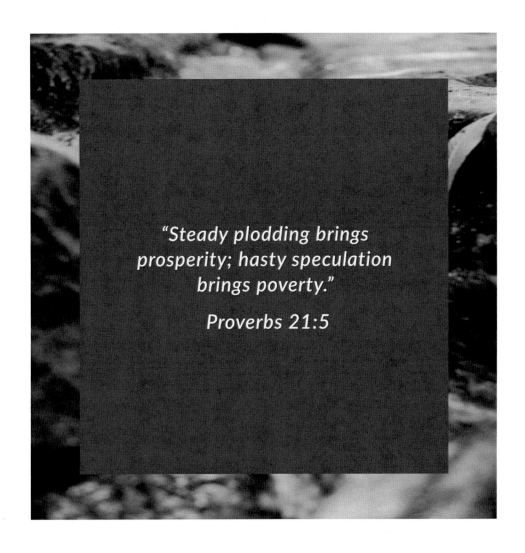

"Steady plodding brings prosperity; hasty speculation brings poverty."

Proverbs 21:5

FOLLOW-UP

How did you do on your tiny financial goal this week?

_____

_____

PODCAST NOTES

openhandsfinance.com/podcasts

Make Plan   Zero Based Budget
Prioritize
Math - Do it

PODCAST RECAP

- ◇ Making a plan for your finances is WISE.
- ◇ Know how much money is coming in and how much is going out.
- ◇ Make a budget with your take-home pay.
- ◇ Live below your means.

QUESTIONS

On a scale of 1-10, how boring does budgeting seem?

◇ ◇ ◇ ◇ ◇ ◇ ◇ ◇ ◇ ◇

SNORESVILLE

HEY, THIS IS
KINDA FUN!

Do you (or did your family) do any kind of budgeting?

_____

_____

_____

_____

_____

_____

_____

How do you currently decide how to spend the money that you make?

_Budget_____

_____

_____

_____

_____

_____

What are three things you want to purchase in the future?

_Land_____—$30,000 - $100,000_____

_Children_____—$20,000_____

_Reliable Car___—$10,000_____

_____

_____

_____

DISCUSSION

Discuss the questions above. Share as much or as little as you're comfortable with.

CASE STUDY

Time for a case study! In today's edition, you'll meet Sam and his budget (and then you'll get to tell Sam what you think he should do!).

SAM
22 YEARS OLD, BUSINESS ANALYST

LOCATION	SALARY	GIVING	RETIREMENT	TAKE-HOME	SPENDING
Portland, OR	$55K	$300/Month	$458/Month	$2,284/Month	No idea!

Sam recently moved to Portland, Oregon for a job as a business analyst. He's making decent money at a job he doesn't mind (win!). Sam contributes 10% of his income to his company's 401K, and they add an additional 4% of free money for future old Sam (lots of employers will do this). Aside from his retirement savings, Sam gives $300 a month to his church and doesn't really pay attention beyond that. He actually has no idea how much money he spends each month but does pay attention so his checking account doesn't totally drain. In terms of lifestyle, Sam has a car but typically bikes everywhere, and he rents a studio apartment in a trendy, walkable neighborhood of Portland. He likes to travel on the weekends and go out to drinks with friends.

When Sam finally sits down and figures out how much money he is spending each month, it turns out he's started spending more than he earns and is slowly draining his little savings nest egg by about $50/month (whoops!). The opposite page shows what Sam's budget currently looks like.

So, Sam needs to trim his budget and asks for your help. Remember, what you would trim and what Sam would trim are likely pretty different. What kind of questions would you ask Sam to help figure out where cuts would fit best?

_____

_____

_____

_____

_____

If you were Sam, where would you start?

_____

_____

_____

_____

_____

FREEDOM in BUDGET
TITHE

SALARY		$55,000
TOTAL MONTHLY		**$4,582**
Giving	Church & World Vision	$300
Retirement	10% (employer matches additional 4%)	$458
Taxes / healthcare / boring stuff	Uncle Sam . . .	$1,000
TOTAL TAKE-HOME		**$2,824**
Savings		$0
Rent / mortgage	Tiny studio apartment	$1,150
Utilities / water / garbage / heating		$70
Car insurance		$100
Car payment	Hyundai Elantra	$210
Groceries	Sometimes eats ramen	$350
Cell phone	Older version of iPhone	$60
Internet		$40
Gas / transportation		$70
Eating out	Drinks / apps with friends	$200
Health / fitness	Fitness classes	$150
Student loans		$150
Trips	Camping trips in the summer	$75
Clothing		$50
Fun money	Concert tickets	$50
Subscriptions	Amazon Prime, Netflix	$30
Miscellaneous	Haircut, flat tire, gifts	$120
TOTAL SPENDING		**$2,875**

WHAT HAPPENS

Sam ends up canceling his expensive fitness membership (which was costing $150 a month) and instantly brings his budget to a break-even point. He even tucks away the extra money to savings to build up three months of living expenses. He goes a bit further and ends up selling his car because he doesn't actually use it.

All of a sudden, Sam has an extra $650 a month, plus a $2,000 cushion from the money he had into his car.

Rock on, Sam. You just slayed that budget.

TIME FOR THE PRACTICAL

Your turn! Let's give a monthly budget template a go. These are going to be very loose numbers, we just want to give you a starting framework when it comes time to make yours. We're going to help you fill in the biggest expenses, and that will inform your more flexible day-to-day spending.

What is your salary (or how much do you estimate you will make in a year)?

41,500

What is your estimated monthly take-home pay?
If you're not sure, try a rough back-of-the-envelope calculation: take the answer from question 1, divide it by 12, and then multiply by 0.75 to loosely account for what's left after taxes.

2,590

How much do you pay in rent or a mortgage?
If you're a student, try looking up the cost of an apartment in the place you want to live and divide if you plan on getting a roommate or two.

1,000

Do you have any debts? What are your monthly payments?
For student loan debt, if you aren't sure, you can use $350 a month as a fill-in for now. We'll dig into the actual number next week.

14,250

13,000

QUICK AND DIRTY GUIDE TO HOW MUCH STUFF COSTS

Unless you have an unexplainable, uncontrollable obsession with alligator skin shoes hand-crafted in Italy or some similar spending proclivity, these are rough estimates of monthly costs (from the low end to the high end) for someone making roughly $40K-$70K a year. These are estimates for single people, couples should increase the amounts in the applicable categories accordingly.

RENT/MORTGAGE: $600-$2,200+

If you live in a less expensive area, you might find standalone rents under $600, or you could also find yourself on the low end if you have a roommate. Plan on easily spending over $1,500 if you live in a bigger city, live alone, or live in a highly desirable area (translation: walkable, trendy, cool). The outliers worth mentioning would be living with your parents (free, no shame), or living somewhere like NYC, SoCal, or San Francisco which will cost you closer to $3K+ for a one-bedroom place.

UTILITIES (WATER, SEWER, GARBAGE, HEATING): $60-$200

You will feel like a true adult (and not in a fun way) when you pay your utility bill. You might be on the low end of $60 if you split the bill with a roommate, or if you live somewhere with a generally temperate climate. Expect a higher bill if you live alone, live in a large space, or live somewhere that is naturally prone to white Christmases.

RETIREMENT: $0-$562

You've gotten this far in the workbook so we're just going to tell you one more time: you should save for retirement. Some people don't ($0). 10% of your salary is good, 15% is great. The person saving 15% on $45K a year will be saving $562 towards retirement each month and if this was through a 401K, this would come out pre-tax (so before your take-home pay).

CAR INSURANCE: $90-$150

Car insurance rates vary widely by state, what kind of car you have, what kind of driver you are or have been, and your age. Expect lower rates for driving boring cars or living in Maine (no joke). High rates typically follow with poor driving records, new expensive cars, and no-fault insurance states like Michigan. Car insurance is usually bundled together in 3-6 month payments, but we've broken it out by month to give you a better idea of month-to-month costs.

CAR PAYMENT: $120-$800

Not everyone will have a car payment, but if you do: it will likely be closer to $120 on the low end for basic cars, all the way up to $800 a month or more for a snazzy new truck or luxury branded car/SUV.

CAR REPAIR: $25-$100

It's when—not if—your car needs some TLC. Bake it into your budget to prevent a rude surprise.

GAS/TRANSPORTATION: $50-$200

If your commute is short or you walk/bike/bus often, you might be on the lower end, while those that have a longer commute or have to pay for daily parking will be on the higher end of the monthly estimate.

GROCERIES: $175-$600

$175 a month will get you a frugal food lineup while $600 will have you eating steaks, organic food, and kefir imported from happy cows. (Remember—these are numbers for a single person. Double it for couples.)

EATING OUT: $20-$400

$20 will get you a couple cheap lunches per month. Frequent eater-outers will quickly find themselves on the higher end of the estimate, especially if dining at swanky bars with cleverly named drinks.

CELL PHONE: $50-$100

If you're still on a family plan or have an older phone, you'll be on the lower end of the spectrum while the unlimited-data-most-recent-phone will be closer to $100 (or more).

INTERNET: $30-$60

Splitting with a roommate will get you closer to $30 while more expensive areas or those with limited internet options will be on the higher end. If you have a cable package, you may be spending $100 a month or more (but who has cable anymore?).

STUDENT LOANS: $0-$600

This one will vary wildly: it just depends on your personal circumstance. In a case of averages, $25,000 in student loans paid over 10 years with a 6.8% interest rate costs $280 a month.

HEALTH/FITNESS: $0-$150

Exercise isn't a priority for everyone ($0). For those with monthly spin classes/Crossfit memberships, expect to pay over $100 a month.

GIVING: $0-$585

While some may choose not to factor giving in, we wholeheartedly recommend you intentionally bake giving into a budget: it's so good for the soul and it's so encouraged in our spiritual life. The biblical description of the tithe is 10%, but whether you give pre-tax or post-tax isn't really a debate worth sparring over. It comes down to your heart (and remember, God doesn't actually need your money, nor can you out-give God).

TRIPS: $0-$600

Travel is expensive but so fun. For those that love trips, keep in mind a weekend away will cost a few hundred dollars while a European jaunt for a week (call it a boot-strapped $1.5K) balances out to $125 a month. Bake this into monthly costs (almost like a subscription!) even if you aren't traveling monthly for the most accurate picture of your real expenses.

CLOTHING: $0-$300

Clothing preferences vary widely. If you love buying clothes (and buying them frequently), you'll be at the higher end of the spectrum or beyond.

SUBSCRIPTIONS: $0-$100

Don't forget about your music subscriptions, delivery subscriptions, video streaming subscriptions, and your monthly box of delight . . . these things are all part of the budget.

MEDICAL: VARIABLE   *280*

Most companies offer health care benefits: some employers cover the whole monthly premium (impressive), but many will cost a few hundred dollars a month taken directly out of your checks. Depending on your health needs, stash some cash on top of your premiums for things like ER visits, surgeries, and the like.

GIFTS: $10-$100

Unless you're Scrooge McDuck, you'll have a few occasions to give gifts. The budget is up to you, but bake this in so you can stress less when you find the perfect gift.

CHRISTMAS: $5-$100

Don't let holiday expenses sneak up on you. Learn this one now and you'll save yourself from the December 26 credit card hangover. $500 in holiday spending will run you about $42/month.

FUN MONEY: VARIABLE

This is a nice budget item after everything else falls into place. Consider this your treat yo'self fund. We've budgeted as low as $50 and as high as $200 in our own setup, but this number is up to you.

MISCELLANEOUS: VARIABLE

This is the junk drawer of a budget. This might be for things like haircuts, household goods, gifts, and so on. A "miscellaneous" category is necessary but it's hard to describe it in averages for this exercise: just know there will be other costs that crop up from month to month. A good starting point might be $100-$150 per month for unexpected expenses.

EXAMPLE BUDGET

Here's another example budget, use it as a reference as you build out your own budget.

SALARY	**$45,000**
TOTAL MONTHLY	**$3,750**
Giving	$375
Retirement	$562
Taxes / healthcare / boring stuff	$703
TOTAL TAKE-HOME	**$2,110**
Rent / mortgage	$550
Utilities / water / garbage / heating	$70
Car insurance	$100
Car payment	$0
Car repair	$25
Gas / transportation	$125
Groceries	$350
Eating out	$70
Cell phone	$60
Internet	$40
Student loans	$150
Health / fitness	$20
Trips	$75
Clothing	$50
Subscriptions	$30
Gifts	$30
Christmas	$40
Fun money	$50
Miscellaneous	$120
TOTAL SPENDING	**$1,955**

YOUR TURN!

Fill in your estimated numbers below.

SALARY	$ 41,500
TOTAL MONTHLY	$ 3450
Giving	$ 345
Retirement	$ 155
Taxes / healthcare / boring stuff	$ 737
TOTAL TAKE-HOME	$ 2,213
Rent / mortgage	$ 1,000
Utilities / water / garbage / heating	$ 100
Car insurance	$ 60
Car payment	$
Car repair	$
Gas / transportation	$ 150
Groceries	$ 350
Eating out	$ 25
Cell phone	$ 50
Internet	$ 50
Student loans	$ 362
Health / fitness	$ —
Trips	$ 20
Clothing	$ 10
Subscriptions	$ 6
Gifts	$ 10
Christmas	$
Fun money	$ 20
Miscellaneous	$
TOTAL SPENDING All of it	$

REVIEW

If your total spending is higher than your take-home pay, that's a problem. Make changes to your spending or earning until you are positive here (this one is a non-negotiable for financial health).

That's it for this week! For the next session, continue to refine your budget until you have a firm idea of the following.

How much money comes in:

_____

How much money goes out:

_____

How much is leftover:

_____

PRACTICAL STEPS THIS WEEK

Track your spending this week using a sheet of paper, notes on your phone, a spreadsheet, or download and try a budget app (I highly recommend using a zero-based budget for the most clarity!).

COMPREHENSION QUESTIONS

1. Who are budgets best for?
   a. Someone who needs to live cheaply
   b. Someone who is just starting out
   c. Someone who has a lot of money
   d. All of the above

2. Which of the following should you include as a line item in your budget?
   a. Loan payments
   b. Vacations
   c. Car repairs
   d. Holiday gifts
   e. All of the above

3. What version on your income is most accurate for determining your budget?
   a. Your salary divided by 12
   b. Monthly take-home pay
   c. Gross monthly income

GOOD JOB COMPLETING
SESSION TWO!

Making a budget can be a hefty undertaking at first, but it will bring so much clarity to your financial decisions.

SAVING
BUILD A CUSHION

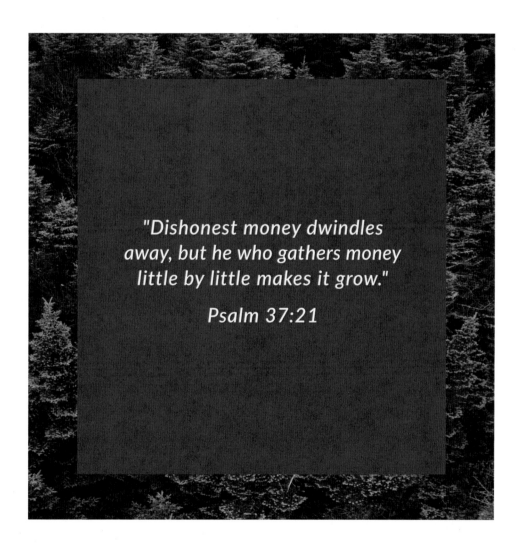

"Dishonest money dwindles away, but he who gathers money little by little makes it grow."

Psalm 37:21

CHECKING IN

How did tracking your spending go? Any surprises?

◆ I tracked my spending   ◆ I didn't track my spending

I was surprised that:

_____

_____

PODCAST NOTES

openhandsfinance.com/podcasts

Emergency fund
Give to God — first fruit
        ↳ God provides

PODCAST RECAP

- ◇ Saving is WISE.
- ◇ As we save, we should first and foremost be rich toward God.
- ◇ The first savings goal is to build up $1,000 in an emergency fund.
- ◇ Saving a cushion is a wise step to do before any aggressive debt payoff.

QUESTIONS

Would you say you're more of a spender or a saver?

◇ ◇ ◇ ◇ ◇ ◇ ◇ ◇ ◇ ◇

SPEND SPEND SPEND   I'M A SAVING PRO

What's a good reason to save?

Did it rock anyone else's world that the point of saving isn't to become wealthy?

_____

_____

_____

_____

_____

_____

Why do you think the Bible instructs us to save only if we are also giving?

Check out the passage from Luke 12:16-21 about the guy who built bigger barns and then died.

Jesus make my brother do what I want

_____

_____

_____

_____

What's the difference between saving and hoarding?

_____

_____

_____

_____

_____

_____

DISCUSSION

Discuss the questions above. Share as much or as little as you're comfortable with.

CASE STUDIES

We've got two case studies this time: one on reducing income and the other on deciding where saved money should go.

DAVID & KATHRYN (WITH BABY GEORGE)

29 YEARS OLD, BUYER | 27 YEARS OLD, INSTRUCTIONAL DESIGNER

LOCATION	SALARY	GIVING	RETIREMENT	TAKE-HOME	SPENDING
Boise, ID	$120K pre-baby $80K post-baby	$680/Month	$1,200/Month	$6,800/Month	$6,500/Month

---

David and Kathryn had a baby recently and life changed in more ways than one. They live in a quaint rambler outside of Boise they bought last year. They're about to reduce their income by $40K a year as Kathryn wanted to go part-time at her job to spend time with baby George (it may be indefinitely, it may not be, they haven't decided yet). Their take-home pay is about to be reduced from $6,800 to $4,600 a month.

How should they handle this transition? What do you think will change in their spending?

_____

_____

_____

_____

_____

_____

_____

_____

_____

_____

_____

WHAT HAPPENS

David and Kathryn dropped their giving and retirement accordingly (now giving $460 and saving $700 a month for retirement). Their house payment remains unchanged, and they actually adjust to a new way of living fairly quickly. They stop the trips to Europe, they eat out far less frequently, and every money decision becomes actually a little easier because baby George just helps set the priority for this simpler way of living (plus baby stuff is expensive!). When the next baby is added to the family, David decides to be a stay-at-home dad when Kathryn wants to go back to work. The couple reduces their expenses even further because they decided that keeping this arrangement was really important to them.

CHRIS & SARA

28 YEARS OLD, SOCIAL WORKER | 26 YEARS OLD, REGISTERED NURSE

LOCATION	SALARY	GIVING	RETIREMENT	TAKE-HOME	SPENDING
Nashville, TN	$110K Combined	$1,100/Month	$1,100/Month	$6,000/Month	$4,500/Month

Chris and Sara have been married for two years and are renting a cute bungalow outside of Nashville. They're giving away 10% of their income and also saving 10% of their income for retirement (with their employers matching the equivalent of 5%). Chris has $35K in outstanding student loans from his master's degree and is on a 10-year loan repayment schedule. The couple has a $1,500 margin each month and they also really want to buy a house.

How should they divvy up the $1,500 they're saving each month? Should they aggressively pay off the loan? Pay the minimum and aggressively save for the house? Or do some of each?

_____

_____

_____

_____

_____

_____

_____

WHAT HAPPENS

Chris and Sara really could've gone either way on this one, but after some long discussions, Chris in particular hated the feeling of being in-debt and they both really valued living debt-free. Chris and Sara started living even further below their means so they could shovel everything extra towards their debt. 18 months later, they paid off the entire amount and are currently living debt-free and are now saving for a down payment on a house.

Note: This scenario gets a little trickier if you're trying to decide between saving for retirement and paying off student loan debts (and buying a house!). If Chris and Sara were in this kind of pickle, it's not exactly a black-and-white decisions and requires some number-crunching and an inventory of what they actually value (being debt-free? Security for the future? Feeling settled?). This would be a great time to talk to a financial planner. There are some solid fee-based planners out there: do make sure they're a fiduciary, which means they're acting with your best interests in mind.

PRACTICAL STEPS THIS WEEK

Pay yourself first. It's an easy and important mantra that will help you build wealth. The easiest way to save is to set up an auto-deduction. When money is deposited into your checking account (like a paycheck), a certain amount gets automatically transferred from your checking account and moved into your savings account. It can be a really small number to get you rolling ($5-$10) or something larger (like 10-20% of your take-home pay). The point is you know how to do it (and you're familiar with how your bank account works).

We highly recommend you set this up but realize some folks won't have the flexibility right now if your bank account is super low. If you decide not to set up a transfer, try sending a calendar invite to yourself for three months as a reminder to do this then.

Set up an automatic savings deduction:

1.   Log into your bank account.

2.   Set up an automatic transfer from checking to savings that repeats once a month. (Don't do this if you're worried about overdraft fees). We would write out specific steps here but every bank is a little different. If needed, call your bank's customer service line for help.

ROTH IRA PART TWO: FUND IT!

While we're at it for boring practical things that make a huge difference, let's revisit your Roth IRA account. Now that you've created your account, the next step will be to fund it.[1] This is step two of three for Roth IRA creation and we'll be going over investing your money in the next session.

Fund your account:

1. This means you're connecting your bank account to your Roth IRA account provider so money can transfer between the two. If you're part of a larger bank, this should be a fairly easy process. If you are part of a smaller bank, this may be slightly more involved.

2. We're asking you to fund $100 into your account (if $100 is tough, try asking a friend or family member to match $50). You're taking care of your future self. You'll thank yourself later.

3. We also strongly recommend setting up a monthly automatic transfer ($20 a month is a great place to start) from your bank account to your Roth IRA account.

4. If you run into any hiccups, reach out to your account provider's customer service team.

1 Want to see it step-by-step? Check out the Roth IRA playlist on the Open Hands TikTok account: @openhandsfinance

COMPREHENSION QUESTIONS

1. If you have $100 in a savings account earning 1% interest, how much would you have after two years?
   a. More than $102
   b. Exactly $102
   c. Less than $102
   d. I don't know, the bank will just tell me

2. Now with your interest rate of 1%, let's say the inflation rate is 5%. After one year, how would that affect the purchasing power of the money in your account?
   a. The money would have more purchasing power compared to today
   b. The money would have less purchasing power compared to today
   c. The money would have the same purchasing power compared to today

3. What is generally considered a good starting point for an emergency fund?
   a. $500
   b. $1,000
   c. $2,000
   d. $5,000

THAT WRAPS UP OUR SESSION ON SAVING

Thanks for joining!

DEBT
DE-STRESS YOUR DEBT

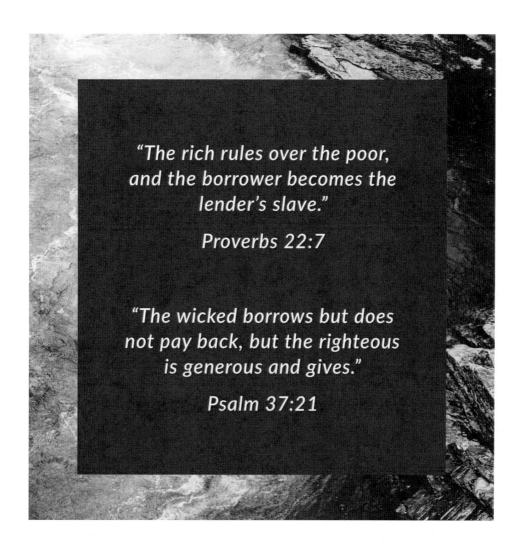

"The rich rules over the poor, and the borrower becomes the lender's slave."

Proverbs 22:7

"The wicked borrows but does not pay back, but the righteous is generous and gives."

Psalm 37:21

CHECK-IN

Did you set up an automatic savings transfer?

◇ Yes   ◇ Not yet

PODCAST NOTES

openhandsfinance.com/podcasts

_____

_____

_____

_____

_____

_____

_____

_____

_____

_____

_____

_____

_____

_____

_____

_____

_____

_____

_____

_____

_____

_____

_____

PODCAST RECAP

◇ Realize the cost of debt (both financial and otherwise) before taking new loans out.

◇ Scriptural debt occurs when we borrow money and cannot pay it back.

◇ Credit cards carry insanely high interest rates: which is why credit card debt is so sludgy.

◇ For those with debt, the first step is knowing how much you have. Then prioritize and work through it. Lots of people do this every day: you can too.

QUESTIONS

What was/is your family's attitude toward debt? What is *your* attitude toward debt?

_____

_____

_____

_____

_____

_____

_____

_____

If you have debt, do find it hard to talk about debt? Why or why not?

_____

_____

_____

_____

_____

_____

_____

_____

Do you think all debt is bad? Can debt be good? Is it neutral? Where or how do you draw the line?

Credit card $10,000 — 100/month

Stress

_____

_____

_____

_____

_____

_____

_____

DISCUSSION

Discuss the questions above. Share as much or as little as you're comfortable with.

AN IMPORTANT PERSPECTIVE ON DEBT

Interest on loans does cost you money, sure, but you're paying for time—time to pay the money back. Take student loans as an example. You want to go to school, but heck if you have the money up front as an 18-year-old! So, you borrow money in the form of student loans, and by paying interest on that loan, you're paying for time to repay it. Knowing the price you pay for that time helps frame the decision more practically.

Take this student loan balance of $30,000 at 5.8% interest over 10 years:

Each month you'll pay about $330. By the end of 10 years, you'll have paid $39,606 in total, with $9,606 of that in interest. Sure, it would be nice to keep that money, but if $9,600 is the difference between affording college and not affording college, it seems like an OK deal.

But interest can also hurt. Take a $3,000 credit card balance at 22% interest. If you just carry that balance of $3,000 and finally pay it off five years later, you'll pay $4,900 total, with $1,900 going to interest.

And if you pay only the $35 minimum, the balance would never get paid off.

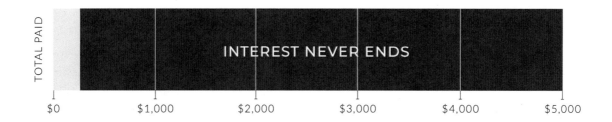

CASE STUDY

This case study gets into how to make a plan for prioritizing when you have a stack of debts/loans.

JAMIE
25 YEARS OLD, MARKETING ANALYST

LOCATION	SALARY	GIVING	RETIREMENT	TAKE-HOME	SPENDING
Atlanta, GA	$50K	$0/Month	$0/Month	$2,800/Month	$2,900/Month

Jamie makes decent money as a marketing analyst and lives in a townhouse she shares with two other roommates. She is paying back student loans, has a car lease, some credit card debt, loves traveling, and frequently goes out with her friends. She has an emergency fund cushion, but does sometimes have to wait for a paycheck before she can pay her bills. She avoids thinking or talking about money, her family never did growing up, and when she does look at her bank account she gets really stressed.

She finally just decides one day she's tired of living like this. She ends up talking to a trusted friend about her situation and the friend helps her make a plan.

If you were Jamie's friend and she came to you, where would you start?
If you ever have friends reach out to you to help with their financial situations, that's a big deal! It means they very much trust you around this sensitive subject.

OUR THOUGHTS

While there are a few routes you could take with Jamie, we would first try to get a quick win to get her inflow and outflow in the positive. It turns out she's spending a lot of money on clothes each month so once we cut that out completely for a few months, this flips her outflow from negative to positive, if only slightly. The good news is she still has about $1000 in an emergency fund so while she is in debt, she's not totally broke.

The next thing we do is make a plan so her debt doesn't feel so overwhelming. We dig into the loan details and they're listed out here. How would you prioritize?

PRIORITY	CREDITOR	PRINCIPLE BALANCE ($)	INTEREST RATE (%)	MINIMUM PAYMENT
	Golden Brain Student Loan	$24,652	6.8%	$300
	Sparkles Credit Card	$1,648	24%	$25
	Tow Mater Car Loan	$12,230	4%	$250
	Tarjay Empire	$458	22.9%	$25

Here's an example prioritizing with the snowball method (paying the lowest balance first to build momentum quickly):

PRIORITY	CREDITOR	PRINCIPLE BALANCE ($)	INTEREST RATE (%)	MINIMUM PAYMENT
1	Tarjay Empire	$458	22.9%	$25
2	Sparkles Credit Card	$1,648	24%	$25
3	Tow Mater Car Loan	$12,230	4%	$250
4	Golden Brain Student Loan	$24,652	6.8%	$300

WHAT HAPPENS

Jaime starts tackling her credit card debt with the smallest balance to build momentum and wipes it out with the next paycheck. Next, she tackles the other credit card (all while paying only the minimums on the other loans). She ends up picking up some freelance work as a blogger while continuing to trim her budget and is on track to pay off all of her credit card debt four months from now. When her car gets a flat tire, she just dips into her emergency fund (which she left intact rather than liquidate for her credit card debt) and her debt repayment plan and savings continue on as usual.

PRACTICAL STEPS THIS WEEK—THOSE WITH DEBT

First step: know what debt you have. We're looking for amounts, location, minimum payment, and interest rate. Write them all down. Having loans, especially as a student or recent student, is simply a reality for lots of us, and we don't want to make that a shameful thing. Acknowledge there is debt, make a plan for repaying, and then start working toward payoff.

CREDITOR	PRINCIPLE BALANCE ($)	INTEREST RATE (%)	MINIMUM PAYMENT
Example: Credit Card 1	$1,235	24%	$25
Example: Student Loan 1	$13,743	4.45%	$50
Student Loan	14,250	4.65%	

With the list above, make a debt snowball plan:

◇ Prioritize your debt either from lowest balance to highest balance, or by highest interest rate to lowest interest rate (for a little mental motivation, go from lowest balance to highest balance).

◇ Add up all the money you are currently paying towards your monthly debts. Subtract out monthly minimum payments for every other debt aside from Priority #1. This amount is now your debt super soaker.

◇ Apply that big debt super soaker of repayment money to Priority #1 until you've paid it off.

◇ Once Priority #1 is paid off, do a little happy dance.

◇ Take your debt super soaker (the full amount), and move on to Priority #2.

◇ Repeat until you've paid off your debts.

◇ Upon debt repayment, or at any celebratory moment along the way, go get a big ol' milkshake and drink it all. Or go on a vacation. Great work.

If you're still in school, it might not be time yet for aggressive repayment (because you likely aren't bringing in a paycheck), but for those that are ready to tackle the beast, there are lots of great online debt snowball calculators a quick Google search away. We also highly recommend checking out Dave Ramsey's *Financial Peace* course for those feeling crippled by debts.

PRACTICAL STEPS THIS WEEK—THOSE WITHOUT DEBT

If you don't have any loans or debt (namely credit card debt), that's neat! It's a rare thing to be free of debt, and whether that's because of your hard work and decisions, financial privilege, or a little bit of both, you've got a unique opportunity in front of you to get ahead and stay ahead.

Whether someone paid for college, you got a scholarship, or you schlepped through paying it all yourself, chances are there might be a thank-you worth expressing. This week, your task is to express your gratitude to someone (maybe it's you!) that helped you get to the spot you are today.

COMPREHENSION QUESTIONS

4. Let's say you have two credit cards, both with a balance of $1,200. Your Chase Emerald card has an interest rate of 19% and your Capital Crunch One has an interest rate of 26%. Which card should you pay off first?
   a. Chase Emerald
   b. Capital Crunch One
   c. Doesn't matter, either one

5. You're about to buy a car and the dealer offers you the same car with either a $225/month payment, or a $325/month payment. What's the catch for the lower payment?
   a. You will pay more in interest over the life of the loan because it's a longer term
   b. You'll pay off the remaining balance in a balloon payment
   c. There's no catch, it's just a good deal

6. What is the difference between principal and interest on a loan?
   a. Principal is the original loan amount, interest is cost to borrow the money
   b. Principal gets paid first, interest rate gets paid second
   c. Interest gets paid first, principal gets paid second

THAT'S IT FOR THIS WEEK'S SESSION ON DEBT

Thanks for joining! Don't forget to give your goals some love this week.

INVESTING
MAKE MONEY WORK FOR YOU

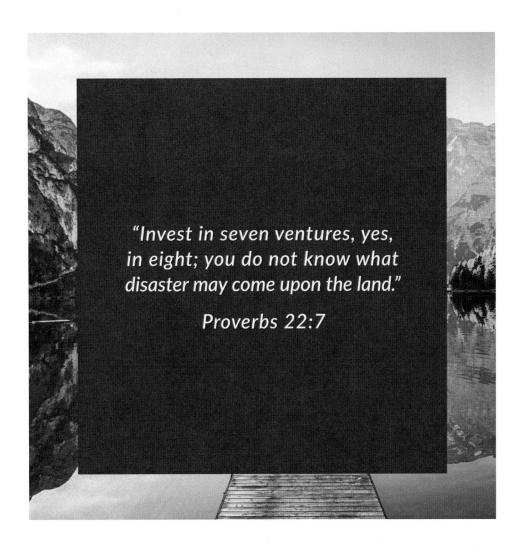

"Invest in seven ventures, yes, in eight; you do not know what disaster may come upon the land."

Proverbs 22:7

CHECKING IN

Did you make a plan for your debt?

◆ Yes   ◆ Not yet

Did you express your gratitude to someone who has helped you?

◆ Yes   ◆ Not yet

PODCAST NOTES

openhandsfinance.com/podcasts

Not a source of stress
As soon as possible
On purpose
1 share = x → changes price

Index fund — Mutual fund   Index — measure (S&P)
Diversify   LP mirror
Small cap   Cheap, Predictable, Diverse
mid cap
large cap (blue chip)
international

PODCAST RECAP

Principles of investing:

◇ Investments shouldn't be a source of stress for you or your budget
◇ Start investing for retirement as early as you can
◇ If you can't afford to lose it, don't invest
◇ Invest with purpose
◇ Be patient
◇ Diversify

QUESTIONS

Have you ever invested before?

_____
_____
_____
_____
_____
_____

Do you feel like you grasp basic groundwork on how investing works? If not, what's still confusing about investing?

_____
_____
_____
_____
_____
_____

What's the difference between a Roth IRA and a 401K (or 403b)?

_____
_____
_____
_____
_____
_____

Bonus question: do you know the difference between a regular IRA and a Roth IRA?

_____
_____
_____
_____
_____
_____

DISCUSSION

Discuss the questions above. Share as much or as little as you're comfortable with.

CASE STUDY

This case study looks at spending decisions of a couple on the higher end of the income spectrum, making 150K/year combined. This may seem like a high number, but for two working college graduates it's not that uncommon.

TIM & BRITTA
31 YEARS OLD, CHEF | 28 YEARS OLD, ATTORNEY

LOCATION	SALARY	GIVING	RETIREMENT	TAKE-HOME	SPENDING
Madison, WI	$150K Combined	$1,250/Month	$1,250/Month	$8,750/Month	$7,000/Month

Tim and Britta are doing well, both in solid jobs and living in a cottage in Madison. They give generously and save toward retirement. Each month, they have $1,750 left over. It's been accumulating in their checking account and they have well over six months of living expenses stored away.

What should Tim and Britta do with the extra money?

_____

_____

_____

_____

_____

_____

_____

_____

_____

_____

_____

WHAT HAPPENS

Although Tim and Britta are living in what seems to be an enviable position, it could be a reality for many of you. Tim and Britta ended up shoveling $800 more a month into their mortgage to pay it off sooner, started socking away $200 a month into a health savings account (for a baby in the future), and put the other $700 a month into their investment account to save for a bigger house for when their family grows. But life throws curve balls, and when having a baby turned out to be much harder than expected, they were thankful to have already saved a cash cushion that would now be going to fertility treatments or adoption instead of spent on a house as their priorities changed.

Another question about Tim and Britta: If they could live on $6,000 a month instead of $7,000 a month, should they try to reduce their living expenses?

_____

_____

_____

_____

_____

_____

_____

_____

If they already tithe 10%, do you think they should give more? Why or why not?

_____

_____

_____

_____

_____

_____

_____

_____

Note: these are all great discussions to have but don't talk too long. We've got some investing to do!

PRACTICAL STEPS THIS WEEK

Okay, so you have a Roth IRA account, it's funded with some dollars, and now it's time to invest. This might sound big and scary at first, but it can be boiled down pretty simply.[1]

ROTH IRA PART THREE: INVESTING YOUR MONEY

1. Get familiar with the lingo
   a. You're going to see all sorts of potentially confusing codewords—those are the stock tickers, or the fund names. These are things like:
      i. TSLA, AMZN, AAPL (individual company stocks)
      ii. VFTAX, FSKAX, VTI, QQQ, VTWO (index funds)
      iii. Fidelity Freedom 2065® Fund, Vanguard Target Retirement 2060 Fund, Fidelity Freedom Index 2060 Fund (target year retirement funds)

2. Know the cost to own the fund
   a. Each fund will have an expense ratio listed. That's the cost to won the fund. These don't get billed to you, but just taken out of the return on the fund. While they seem small and piddly now, as your account balances grow, these amounts can really add up.
      i. Expense ratio: 0.02%—that means every $1,000 would charge $0.02 annually
      ii. Expense ration: 0.5%—that means every $1,000 invested would cost $5 annually
      iii. Expense ration 1.5%—that means every $1,000 invested would cost $15 annually

3. Look at investing minimums
   a. We're starting as small fries, so look for funds with $0 investing minimums.

4. Look at cost of fund. If it's more than what you have, can you buy partial shares? And remember—more expensive shares do not mean better shares.

5. Decide on a fund

6. Time to trade!
   a. Trading means you're buying investments. You'll enter your symbol, choose "buy" and you can either purchase by shares or by dollars. Since we're limited more by dollars, you'll have to do less math that way. Enter the purchase amount you want and then you'll see two buying choices:
      i. Market: you'll buy at the next market price
      ii. Limit: you choose to set the threshold of paying no more than $X amount of dollars per share.
      It's easiest and fastest to buy at market price, but knowing the limit option is helpful for future investing.

7. Find something that works and invest!
   a. Neat, you did it!
   b. Set up a calendar reminder for 6-8 months from now to reevaluate your retirement account: can you increase your monthly funding? Are your options diversified?

---

1 Want to see a closer look at investing money in a Roth IRA? Check out the Roth IRA playlist on TikTok @openhandsfinance

Sometimes the market will go up. Sometimes it will go down. But historically, investments have been like a yo-yo going uphill. Over the long term, the stock market has averaged 10% returns. That means if you have $1,000 invested, after one year it will have earned $100 without doing a single thing. Some years you'll have an amazing eye-popping 20% return, and some years will be a nail-biting -50% dip. Yep, at some point, you will experience a market drop. Chances are very, very high it will go up, but there are no guarantees, and that's just a reality of investing.

The upside is that if you stack enough return-earning years on top of each other, your money will start to compound in an exponential curve that's practically impossible to wrap your head around.

EXAMPLE ROTH IRA PROJECTION[2]

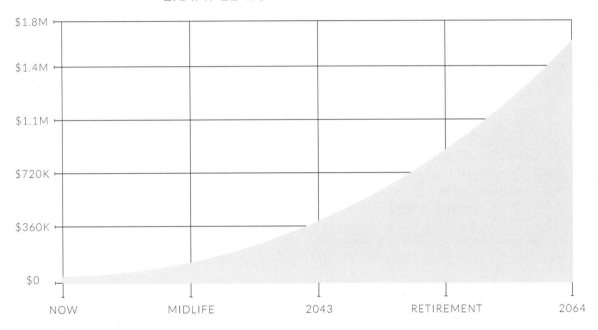

$1.63 MILLION
EXAMPLE ROTH IRA BALANCE AT RETIREMENT

$100	$50/MONTH	$500/MONTH	7%
Initial contribution funded at age 20	Amount funded from ages 20-22	Amount funded from age 23+	Rate of return on investments

2 This is a projection based on historical returns, but we're not saying by any means this is a guaranteed return.

HOW DO I PICK WHAT FUND I WANT TO INVEST IN?

We can't give specific fund recommendations because of all sorts of legal things, but when you're looking at retirement accounts like a Roth IRA:

- ◇ AVOID individual company stocks. Very risky.
- ◇ It's worked well for us to invest in low-cost index funds to keep more of your money over the long run.
- ◇ For the most hands-off, don't-have-to-know-much-about-investing or pay attention all the time, some people will like Target Date retirement funds. They are a little more expensive, but they're easy-peasy-bo-beasy.

A peek into our retirement account strategy:

- ◇ When I started my Roth IRA at age 21, I just made my best guess, set up automatic investments, and then didn't look at it much over the next few years. It was the right thing for me at that time, to just get started.
- ◇ In my mid-twenties, I got a little more confidence and learned a little more about investing. My money had grown, but I was in some higher cost mutual funds that I decided to dump. It was the right thing at the right time, to take some time to understand investing more and tweak the portfolio.
- ◇ Today, we have a handful of retirement funds, and they're a mix of low-cost index funds and target retirement funds. Now that we've had a decade of wealth-building and managing a larger portfolio, we set up time with a financial advisor to do a thorough comb-through and tidy up our allocations. That feels like the right thing for this time, to get an expert opinion, refine, and optimize.
- ◇ I look at our portfolio balances once a month when I do the rest of our monthly financial check-up. There have been times that I look at it once a year. For us, looking less means less stress. We're not planning to use the money for decades yet, so looking and stressing doesn't help any.

All that to say, you don't have to feel like you need to get everything about investing right away. What we've found (and what many others have found), is that more important than picking the most high-performing fund is to invest consistently over time, and to start as early as you can.

COMPREHENSION QUESTIONS

1. Which retirement vehicle gets funded with after-tax dollars?
    a. Roth IRA
    b. 401K
    c. 403B
    d. Traditional IRA

2. How much can you contribute to your Roth IRA?
    a. Up to the amount of your earned income, up to the yearly cap
    b. $5,000/year
    c. Any amount
    d. However much you plan to make this year

3. In looking at possible investments, one fund has an expense ration of 1.1% and another has an expense ration of 0.18%. Which fund is cheaper to own (assuming all other fees are equal)?
    a. 1.1%
    b. 0.18%

CONGRATS

You did it!

EVERYDAY MONEY HABITS
FINANCIAL DECISION-MAKING

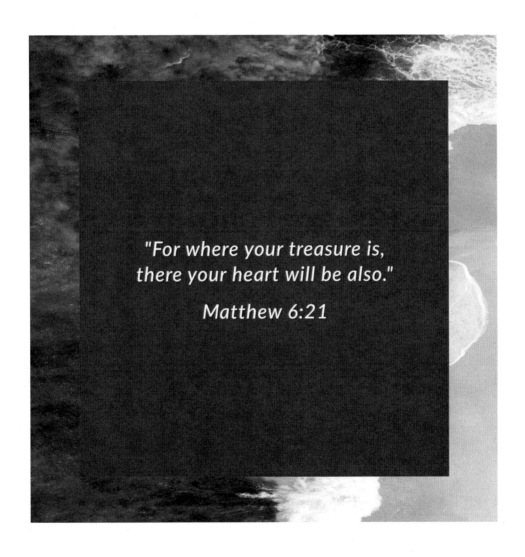

*"For where your treasure is,
there your heart will be also."*

Matthew 6:21

CHECKING IN

Were you able to invest your Roth IRA money?

◆ Yes   ◆ Not yet

PODCAST NOTES

openhandsfinance.com/podcasts

_____

_____

_____

_____

_____

_____

_____

_____

_____

_____

_____

_____

_____

_____

_____

_____

_____

PODCAST RECAP

◇ Be gentle with your financial expectations of yourself (especially when you're young). It's ok not to live in a swanky place! It's ok if you don't buy coffee and go to happy hour all the time! It's ok to drive an old car!

◇ In the next few years, you're setting the money habits for the rest of your life. Choose carefully.

◇ The time to set your course for generosity is now, not later.

◇ Try not to judge or compare yourself to others' financial choices. You'll rarely have the full picture and priorities are SO different.

◇ Those around you will often dictate your standard of living.

◇ Be wary of lifestyle creep.

◇ Talk about financial matters and topics with people who you trust and are wise.

◇ If you're in a serious relationship, we encourage you to talk openly about financial matters (though do be both well-rested and well-fed beforehand). It's good for your relationship.

QUESTIONS

What do you imagine your life will be like a few years from now? What does your place look like? What does your neighborhood look like? What does your car look like? Write it out so you see what expectations you have for yourself!

Small house (1 bd)

Same car

Basement?

Part time HVAC?

What money habits do you want to have?

Intentional   _Don't let it rule your life_

"Paying myself first"

Not living paycheck to paycheck

Emergency Fund

What habits do you want to change?

Pay self from savings first

Consistent hours

What current habits, actions, or mindsets do you currently have that you want to keep?

Simple life

Reduce/Reuse/recycle

From scratch

Who could you talk to about financial matters that you trust?

Eric / Jonathan & Hannah

DISCUSSION

Discuss the questions above. Share as much or as little as you're comfortable with.

AN IMPORTANT THING TO KEEP IN MIND ABOUT FINANCIAL HABITS

We all start in different spots financially at the beginning of our earning years.

- ◇ You might have giant student loans to pay off
- ◇ You might be digging out from money decisions you wish you hadn't made
- ◇ You might have $300 in the bank
- ◇ You might have $3,000 in the bank
- ◇ You might have $3 in the bank

And yes, it's easy to compare and complain about how it's just not fair, but you know how the saying goes: that's life. Life isn't fair. There's good news: you just have to worry about you. Your financial life could sort out any number of ways, and a lot of that is well within your control based on the financial decisions that you make.

To illustrate , look at these three paths, all possibilities for you, and all starting from the same place.

PATH ONE

You graduate and just don't do much of anything. You might save money if there's any left over at the end of the month (not usually), you pay the minimums on your loans, and you just don't pay much attention to where your money goes. You're just living life! After five years, you're basically where you started, maybe just a little better.

PATH TWO

You graduate and start living just a little large. You're not saving anything (you've got time!), you're not tackling debt (you've got time!), you don't have margin (you're young!), and you're relying on credit to get you through to your next paycheck. After five years, you're actually worse off than when you started.

PATH THREE

You graduate and try to make good money moves. You're paying yourself first (if only a little), you're living below your means (there's money still left between paychecks, a little more each time), and you're paying a little extra on your loans each month. After five years, you're seriously ahead!

CASE STUDY

SCOTT
22 YEARS OLD, CUSTOMER SERVICE REPRESENTATIVE

LOCATION	SALARY	GIVING	RETIREMENT	TAKE-HOME	SPENDING
Charlotte, NC	$28K	$200/Month	$200/Month	$1,286/Month	$1,200/Month

Scott is currently working as a customer service representative in Charlotte and, to be perfectly honest, he knows he doesn't have a ton of wiggle room in his budget. Between social outings with friends, eating lunches out, Scott has to be careful in how he spends his money so he doesn't overspend each month. When he comes up for a promotion at work (and a $3,000 pay raise), the first thing he wants to do is to trade in his college car that's going on 10 years old and has a few more clunks than it used to for a new lease on an affordable, dependable Honda.

Should Scott buy a new car? Why or why not?

_____

_____

_____

_____

_____

_____

_____

_____

_____

_____

_____

_____

WHAT HAPPENS

Scott took a few minutes to crunch numbers (the $3K pay raise got him an extra $200 a month after taxes) and decide what was actually important to him. He wanted to have his finances in good shape, and he realized the new car lease would keep him in the same financial position of cutting it close each month that he didn't enjoy that much. He decided to keep his college car for at least another year and a half (and committed to the repair costs as well), at which point he planned on reevaluating a new-to-him car purchase.

CASE STUDY

QUINN & SHAWN
31 YEARS OLD, INTERIOR DESIGNER | 29 YEARS OLD, DEVELOPER

LOCATION
Seattle, WA

SALARY
$140K Combined

GIVING
$800/Month

RETIREMENT
$1,500/Month

TAKE-HOME
$7,800/Month

SPENDING
$7,500/Month

Quinn and Shawn have solid jobs and love living in Seattle. They really want to buy a house, but even a started home in the area they want to live costs a half-million dollars. They only have a 5% down payment ($25K on a $500K house) but would still love to be homeowners. They just paid off Quinn's student loans ($300/month) and will have Shawn's paid off in three years ($400/month).

Should Quinn and Shawn buy a $500,000 house? Why or why not?

_____
_____
_____
_____
_____

What would some benefits of renting be for Quinn and Shawn? What about buying a house?

_____
_____
_____
_____
_____

If you were in their situation, what would you do?

_____
_____
_____
_____
_____

WHAT HAPPENS

The couple ends up moving further out from the city and finding a house for $450,000. They qualify for a first-time homeowner loan and are able to put about 5% down ($25,000) and are paying slightly more each month than they were for rent. The house isn't their dream home and needs some renovations, but it has a lock-off basement that they rent out for extra income. After a few years, the hour-long commute takes its toll and the couple ends of selling the house for a healthy profit and move a few hours away to a more affordable area (with Shawn working remotely and Quinn finding a new job) for the next chapter or life.

PRACTICAL STEPS THIS WEEK

You'll be writing out three things you want to do in the next year in terms of your finances. Write it in a note on your phone, an email to yourself, on an index card, or on this page. Just somewhere you'll be able to look at from time to time and check how you're doing.

GOAL #1

What is a WISE financial goal you'd like to accomplish? I want to . . .
Examples: up my ROTH contribution, get out of credit card debt, use a budget app, have $1K in an emergency fund, keep driving my college car, etc.

Pay off school before graduating

GOAL #2

What is a GENEROUS financial goal you'd like to accomplish? I want to . . .
Examples: start tithing, find a non-profit I support to start giving to, buy someone coffee, be hospitable, live with an open hands mindset, volunteer somewhere, etc.

Support missionary w/ tithe

GOAL #3

What is a PERSONAL finance goal you'd like to accomplish? I want to . . .
Examples: save enough money to travel around Europe, pay off one of my loans, go visit a friend who lives far away, be able to afford (and then buy) that dreamy _____ I really want, be self-sustaining with a job, move somewhere awesome, etc.

Go to Fulda

Write it all down. Keep it somewhere where you can reference it. Remind yourself in a few months these are the things you are aiming for. This is how you want to live your life.

COMPREHENSION QUESTIONS

1. How much money will you need saved to put 10% down on a $350,000 house?
    a. $35,000 plus first and last payments
    b. $35,000 plus closing costs
    c. $3,500 plus taxes and fees
    d. $35,000 plus closing costs and $3,500 for first-year repairs

2. How much cash do you need to hand over for first, last, and a $500 deposit on a $1,400/month apartment?
    a. $2,800
    b. $4,200
    c. $3,300
    d. $3,500

3. Which of the following financial rules-of-thumbs will generally make your wealth grow?
    a. Spend less than you earn
    b. Pay yourself first
    c. Save 20% of your income
    d. All of the above

4. By how much does the average college student overestimate their starting salary?
    a. $5,000
    b. $10,000
    c. $15,000
    d. $50,000

THAT'S IT!

Go forth and live your life as a wise steward and generous human being. Thank you SO much for joining.

MANAGING MONEY AS A COUPLE
BONUS SESSION

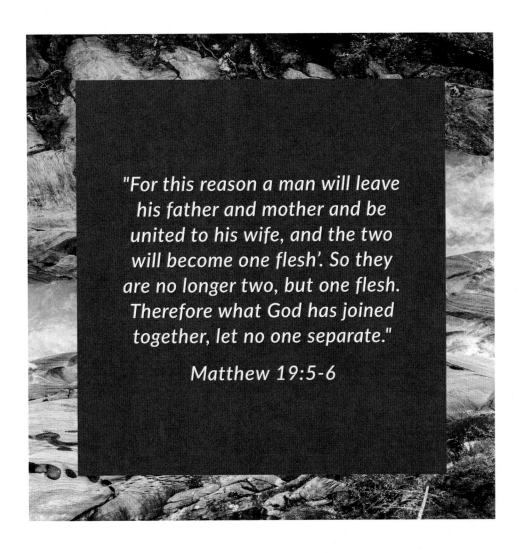

"For this reason a man will leave his father and mother and be united to his wife, and the two will become one flesh'. So they are no longer two, but one flesh. Therefore what God has joined together, let no one separate."

Matthew 19:5-6

PODCAST NOTES

openhandsfinance.com/podcasts

_____
_____
_____
_____
_____
_____
_____
_____
_____
_____
_____
_____
_____
_____
_____
_____
_____

PODCAST RECAP

The money rules from the couple mentioned in the podcast, written out: (and to re-iterate, these rules will be different for everyone, we just want to give an example as a starting point).

- ◇ Agree that neither of you can make a purchase above $75 without first consulting the other.
- ◇ Agree that there will be no secret bank accounts, no earnings that are not disclosed, no undisclosed loans and no secret credit cards.
- ◇ Join all your finances together.
- ◇ It should take two "Yeses" for any major financial decision.
- ◇ Budget will be strictly adhered to, except in cases of emergency.
- ◇ Budget will be reviewed at the end of each month.
- ◇ If fun money has been spent, it is spent. There will be no arguing, pouting, name-calling or fighting.
- ◇ Fun money does not have to be spent in that month and may be carried over. There is no borrowing against future months.
- ◇ A car fund will be established and money—no less than $50—placed into it every pay period, to be reviewed after three months. (Or a house fund, or a vacation fund, you get the idea.)
- ◇ $400 ($200 each) in "magic money" will be allotted out of bonuses, with the rest going to either long-term needs or savings.

QUESTIONS

Here are some questions to go over with your partner. Two rules before you can talk about them:

1. You must not be hungry.

2. You must not be tired.

These are difficult questions in any situation so set yourself up for success by taking care of those two essentials. If you are either, go eat something, go take a nap, or do both! These questions will be here when you're ready. Feel free to write them out first or talk your way through them: whatever works best for you.

Do you err on the side of spending or saving?

_____
_____
_____
_____
_____

What side do you think I err on and why?

_____
_____
_____
_____
_____

How much do you think a vacation should cost?

_____
_____
_____
_____
_____

What's a goal or purchase you want to make (just you!) that requires money?

_____
_____
_____
_____
_____

NOW WE DIG INTO SOME HEAVIER FINANCIAL QUESTIONS

Do you have any undisclosed debts?

_____

_____

_____

_____

_____

Are there any large financial implications in the coming years?
Do you plan on going back to school? Do you want to go on a big vacation or take a gap year?

_____

_____

_____

_____

_____

Is your money combined (or do you plan on combining it)? If not, why?

_____

_____

_____

_____

_____

What's one financial goal we have as a couple?

_____

_____

_____

_____

_____

Do you feel like we're on the same page with our current financial spending?

_____

_____

_____

_____

_____

How much could I spend without telling you?

_____

_____

_____

_____

_____

_____

What's one thing you would change about the way we handle our money?

_____

_____

_____

_____

_____

_____

Do we need to set any new parameters?
Fun money? Spending limits?

_____

_____

_____

_____

_____

_____

What do you appreciate about the way we've handled money so far?

_____

_____

_____

_____

_____

_____

DISCUSSION

Time for a discussion with the above questions. Obviously this time it's just with your partner!

CASE STUDY

This one is less of a "case study" and more of just an awareness of a very common scenario for many couples (maybe yourselves included!). The good news is it's never too late to get on a common page with your partner in terms of your financial goals and start working toward them.

JENNY & GORDON

22 YEARS OLD, BARISTA | 24 YEARS OLD, LOGISTICS COORDINATOR

LOCATION	SALARY	GIVING	RETIREMENT
Denver, CO	$56K Combined	$12/Month	$100/Month

Jenny and Gordon got married last year in a beautiful mountainside ceremony and life was newlywed bliss for a solid year. But lately, Jenny and Gordon have been fighting . . . a lot . . . and it always seems to come down to money. Jenny is a saver, Gordon is a spender, and they often spend on different things. They're currently living check to check, and it's always extra tense at the end of the month as they hope their credit cards don't get declined. It's causing considerable strain on their marriage but they don't have anyone to talk to about it (Gordon's family is awful with money while Jenny's family would never talk about finances openly).

What should they do? Where should they start?

_____
_____
_____
_____
_____
_____
_____
_____
_____
_____
_____
_____
_____
_____
_____
_____

WHAT HAPPENS

The couple ended up hearing about a program through their church that offered financial counseling for couples and hesitantly decided to give it a try. The financial counselor recommended they first and foremost get on the same page in terms of their values. Both Jenny and Gordon really valued financial freedom (and being able to have control over money rather than having their money control their decisions). This was more important than new furniture, trendy restaurants, and new clothes.

Once they established a common shared direction, it became much easier to make changes. They decided they wanted to save three months worth of living expenses in the next year and stop living check to check, so Gordon cut down on his extra spending, Jenny continued to look for ways to save, and the two even ended up switching apartments to a more affordable place.

They still fought about money throughout the year, but it wasn't like it used to be: it wasn't as cutting, it wasn't as mean. By the end of the year, the two were able to save $8K and no longer had to live check to check. They would both say it required a TON of work to get there, and it was often painful, but neither of them regretted the hard conversations and hard decisions to get to a point of financial freedom.

PRACTICAL STEPS

Set your own "money rules". Borrow from the ones listed earlier in the session, make your own, or do a little of both!

◇ _____

◇ _____

◇ _____

◇ _____

◇ _____

◇ _____

◇ _____

◇ _____

◇ _____

◇ _____

◇ _____

◇ _____

◇ _____

◇ _____

◇ _____

◇ _____

APPENDIX A
GENERAL TERMS

401K

What it does: A safe haven for your retirement money. Your money is not taxed until it comes out. Many employers offer "matching" incentives, so if you chip in $300 of your paycheck, your employer will offer to match your contribution. A common match is 50 cents on the dollar, up to roughly 6% of your paycheck (but these numbers vary quite a bit from company to company).

Why you should pick a 401(k): If your employer offers a match, you should definitely contribute to your 401(k) account; it's basically free money. Just be ready to be taxed on it when you take it out. Another great perk of a 401(k) account is the money automatically comes out of your paycheck and is set aside, before you can even miss it.

AUTOMATIC DEDUCTION

Let the robots do your work. Set up automatic deductions to move your money from your paycheck to your retirement account, or set up an automatic transfer to move from checking account to savings account. These can occur weekly, monthly, or on whatever schedule you prefer but it's a wonderful tool to save.

BONDS

Government-issued debt: where you loan them money, and they pay you interest. Generally regarded as super safe, bonds pay a return that's typically lower than investing in the riskier market, but it's virtually guaranteed.

BNPL

Buy now, pay later These are installment loans like Affirm, Klarna, Afterpay—while offering zero percent loans, you can get in a pickle if you get in the habit and stack too many loans up without realizing it.

CRYPTOCURRENCY

Digital currency like Ethereum and Bitcoin that's built on block-chain technology. It's kind of like a digital ledger for information that can be recorded but not edited. It's very volatile as an investment and not something that would normally be part of retirement savings, but it's an interesting Wild West in financial technology.

EMERGENCY FUND

$1,000 in an easy-to-get-to-place. To be used in emergencies. A great idea and buffer against going into debt.

EXCHANGE TRADED FUNDS (ETFS)

ETFs are buckets of assets, also a bit like the mutual fund buffets. However, they are a cheaper, passively managed, and a more transparent version of mutual funds, and many have no investment minimum.

HIGH-YIELD SAVINGS ACCOUNT

A savings account that offers a beefier interest rate than a typical savings account. Think 1% vs 0.05%. You'd earn $1 on $100 vs. $0.05.

APPENDIX B
STUDENT LOAN RESOURCE

Remember when you were 16 and still learning how to make mac and cheese? Then you turned 18 and were allowed to borrow $100,000 to go to college? Yeah, student loans are a little fuffed up. But here we are, making a plan, dealing, because sometimes that's just what you gotta do in life. And figuring out how to deal with student loans is one of those valuable life lessons that no amount of money can teach you. A little grit. A little persistence. A little roll-up-your-sleeves and make it happen. You're going to make money work for you, whatever your situation, and this will serve you well for decades yet to come. First, a little recap.

WHAT ARE STUDENT LOANS?

College isn't cheap. To foot the bill, students and parents can borrow money to pay for school. This money can come from the federal government, who makes loans that sound like this:

◇ Direct subsidized loans
◇ Direct unsubsidized loans
◇ Direct PLUS loans

Glamorous, right? These loans come with flexibility in payment plans, they're relatively easy to get, and they come with federal protections (like when many borrowers got a pause on payments and interest during COVID).

Another source of loans are private sources. This might be from a local credit union, banks like Wells Fargo, servicers like Sallie Mae, heavily-marketed companies like Sofi, or state-affiliated non-profit groups. If you need to borrow a lot of money (such as for an expensive or private college), you might have a mix of both federal and private loans.

With these loans, interest starts accruing while you're still in school eating late-night pizza, but payments won't start until you graduate. You can also think of these loans as that frenemy who is a little extra—you may have been required to have a cosigner if you lacked creditworthiness, student loan debt does not go away in bankruptcy, and in some cases, doesn't even go away upon death. Wow. Yeah.

After borrowing money for college, going to college, and hopefully graduating college, you start paying back money you borrowed in monthly chunks (but if you don't graduate or drop below a certain number of credit hours, you'll still have to start paying back those loans when that happens). Let's get familiar with some numbers:

~$30,000[1]	5.8%[2]	10 YEARS 120 MONTHS	20 YEARS[3]	$448/MONTH[4]
Typical student loan balance at graduation	Average student loan interest rate	Original loan repayment timeline	Time it actually takes the average borrower to repay	Average monthly loan payment for someone with a Bachelor's degree

---

HOW MUCH WILL YOU PAY?
Roughly ~100/month in payment for every $10,000 borrowed.

---

1 https://educationdata.org/average-student-loan-debt-by-year
2 https://educationdata.org/average-student-loan-interest-rate
3, 4 https://educationdata.org/average-student-loan-payment

WHEN DO I START PAYING THEM BACK?

It depends. (For more information on repayment schedules, check out the federal student loan site.[5])

◇ For most federal loans, six months after graduating or when you drop below half-time enrollment.

◇ For PLUS loans (those are the ones parents usually take out), payments would start once the loan has been paid out. If you're a grad student with a PLUS loan, you get an automatic deferment (means the paying back gets pushed out until after graduation).

◇ For private loans, it varies by lender. Some have a grace period until six months after graduation, others start once the loan is dispersed.

WHAT IF I CAN'T AFFORD THE MONTHLY PAYMENT?

Student loan payments do chomp a big mouthful from your monthly take-home pay. They have a big appetite each and every month, and they must be fed. But if you're struggling to make payments, there are some options you can pursue.

One thing you DON'T want to do is stop making payments on Federal loans (unless they're paused). They have deep claws they can sink into your financial life–money could be taken from your wages before you get it, money could be taken straight from your tax return, fees[6] could be issued, and you could even be sued. It's no joke! If you have competing debts all fighting for your money, federal student loans are definitely at the top of the priority list to pay back.

Here's an ordered list of actions you can take (the best option being listed first).

◇ Contact your loan servicer ASAP, explain your situation, and find out your options to avoid defaulting on your student loans.

◇ Switch repayment plans with your servicer. For federal loans, many qualify for a plan that caps payments at 10-20% of your discretionary income. As in, maybe you have $1200 of discretionary income each month, so your loan payment might be $120. Sure, you might end up paying more in interest over the life of the loan, but think of paying this interest as buying time!

◇ Look into consolidation. Federal loan holders can apply for Federal loan consolidation, which keeps many of the privileges of Federal loans, but doing so might limit interest rate discounts or cancellations, so that's a big decision! One thing to be especially wary of is taking your federal loans and consolidating them into a private loan–you might get a lower interest and a simplified monthly payment, but you lose a lot of that cloak of protection and flexibility offered with Federal loans.

◇ Consider forbearance or deferment. If you're dealing with financial hardship, medical expenses, you might have a case to delay loan payments. You'll have to request this with your loan provider, and keep up payments in the meantime while you wait to hear if you're approved.

---

5 https://studentaid.gov/help-center/answers/article/when-do-i-have-to-start-repaying-federal-student-loans
6 https://studentaid.gov/understand-aid/types/loans/interest-rates

WHAT ABOUT PUBLIC SERVICE LOAN FORGIVENESS?

Hey you public servants! If you're working at a non-profit or for the government (maybe you're a social worker, pastor, or in the ministry) and have Direct federal student loans, you may qualify for a special relief program called Public Service Loan Forgiveness (or PSLF for short).

Here's the gist of it:

- ◇ You work full-time for a "qualifying employer" (as in, the government or a non-profit)
- ◇ Go on an income-based repayment plan and settle into making those monthly payments
- ◇ After making on-time payments for 120 months (that's 10 years), the remaining balance on your student loans would be forgiven.

Now, this program has been full of high hopes but full of complexity and disappointment, so do be very careful and read the fine print five times if you're pursuing this option. It did get an overhaul during the pandemic, and is in better shape–but as always, you're your best advocate and plan to track everything on your end.

To see if you qualify, use the PSLF help tool[7] or read more[8] about how the program works on the studentaid.gov site.

HOW DO I FIND MY LOANS?

The studentaid.gov[9] site is the home base for all Federal-related student loans, and that's the best place to start if you're unsure who is the loan servicer on your loans. The school where you graduated will also have this information if you can't find it on the .gov website.

CAN I USE STUDENT LOANS FOR LIVING EXPENSES?

Yes, student loans can be used for things like groceries, housing, laptops, and textbooks. But be aware that every purchase you make with student loan money is costing you more (because of the loan interest), and keep tabs on your balance to make sure you have enough to cover tuition first and foremost!

HOW MUCH CAN I TAKE OUT IN LOANS?

Student loans aren't unlimited, and limits for undergrad Federal loans are much lower than you might think (as in $5,500 total for freshman year). Adding a cosigner can qualify you for additional loans, and private loans can help cover any shortfalls, up to the school's total cost of attendance. But keep in mind, just because you can take out a certain amount in loans doesn't mean you have to!

---

7 https://studentaid.gov/pslf/
8 https://studentaid.gov/manage-loans/forgiveness-cancellation/public-service
9 https://studentaid.gov/h/manage-loans

APPENDIX C
HOW TO BUILD GOOD CREDIT

You know how in high school and college, it's all about that GPA? Well, once you graduate, no one talks about GPA anymore (hate to break it to ya), but everyone talks about credit score. And by everyone, we mean the people from whom you would want to borrow money from for a car loan, home loan, or get approved by a landlord to rent an apartment.

And unlike a GPA, you can't turn in a sparkling paper or do some extra credit to boost your grade. Instead, your credit score is about things like longevity and consistency: like how long you've been borrowing money, and if you make your payments on time.

Here's what the scale looks like, translated roughly in the GPA language you might currently understand:

CREDIT SCORE RATING SCALE

300	400	500	600	700	750	800	850
F	D	C-	C	B	B+	A	A+
Poor	Still Poor	Meh	Fair	Good	Very Good	Exceptional	Perfect

A good credit rating will get you the best interest rate when taking out loans or credit cards. And as a renter, having a good credit score could put you in the front of the line in the landlord's eyes as the person to get the rental spot.

But if you're someone who doesn't have a credit card or has never made any loan payments, a lender would look at you and automatically stamp a failing grade on your report card. See, without a credit score, they see you as a big risk. And they don't like risks when it comes to lending their money.

HOW YOUR CREDIT SCORE IS CALCULATED

- ◇ How many accounts do you have? (*Have you opened a flurry of new accounts recently? Ding. Only one account? Ding.*)
- ◇ What kind of loans do you have (*Lenders sometimes like to see that you can handle multiple types of loans—like static monthly car or student loan payments along with more fluctuating credit card balance payments.*)
- ◇ How much of your available credit do you use? (*Are you using 30% or less of your available balance? That means if your limit is $10,000, you balance never goes above $3,000.*)
- ◇ How long have you been a borrower? (*Longer is better.*)
- ◇ Do you make your payments on time?

In a catch-22, you need to have credit to build credit, but it's hard to get credit if you don't have any. It's the same as when you need experience to get a job or an internship, but it's hard to get any experience when you have no experience. UGH. The never-ending loop.

But, there is a way out! There are a few options to build your credit score.

HIGH FIVE,
YOU DID IT!

Cheers to managing money wisely, blessing and being
blessed by generosity, and stepping into the story laid
out for you without money holding you back.

THE END!

Or is it just the beginning...

Money, tips, and encouragement straight to your inbox.
Sign up for the newsletter at openhandsfinance.com

Add Open Hands Finance on TikTok and Instagram
@openhandsfinance

Like what's been going on in here? Pass it on!
Visit openhandsfinance.com to learn more about bringing this
program to a church, small group, or college near you.

ADDITIONAL NOTES